HAL•LEONARD
WEDDING ESSENTIALS

AUDIO ACCESS INCLUDED

PLAYBACK+
Speed • Pitch • Balance • Loop

WEDDING VIOLIN SOLOS

HAL•LEONARD®
CORPORATION
7777 W. BLUEMOUND RD. P.O. BOX 13819 MILWAUKEE, WI 53213

HL00842456

CAN YOU FEEL THE LOVE TONIGHT

from Walt Disney Pictures' THE LION KING

Violin

Music by ELTON JOHN
Lyrics by TIM RICE

22
24
mf
mp
25
3
28
f
31
35
mp
2
39
mf
rall.
43
Freely
mp
46
a tempo
p
molto rit.

GABRIEL'S OBOE

from the Motion Picture THE MISSION

Violin

Words and Music by
ENNIO MORRICONE

GROW OLD WITH ME

Violin

Words and Music by
JOHN LENNON

HERE, THERE AND EVERYWHERE

Violin

Words and Music by JOHN LENNON
and PAUL McCARTNEY

HIGHLAND CATHEDRAL

Violin

By MICHAEL KORB
and ULRICH ROEVER

I WILL BE HERE

Violin

Words and Music by
STEVEN CURTIS CHAPMAN

32
To Coda
36
D.S. al Coda
CODA
39
40
44
5
52
56
59
63
67
rit.
p

THE LORD'S PRAYER

Violin

By ALBERT H. MALOTTE

27
poco accel.
31
rallentando
a tempo
34
35
37
Poco meno mosso, e sonoramente
rit.
40
43
Tempo I
46
rallentando e morendo

SUNRISE, SUNSET

from the Musical FIDDLER ON THE ROOF

Violin

Words by SHELDON HARNICK
Music by JERRY BOCK

47
53
59
65
D.S. al Coda
CODA
a tempo
71
77
83
85
mp
89
95
rit.

WEDDING PROCESSIONAL

from THE SOUND OF MUSIC

Violin

Lyrics by OSCAR HAMMERSTEIN II
Music by RICHARD RODGERS

YOU RAISE ME UP

Violin

Words and Music by BRENDAN GRAHAM
and ROLF LOVLAND